Unseen Showers

Sana Twinkle

Chennai • Bangalore

CLEVER FOX PUBLISHING
Chennai, India

Published by CLEVER FOX PUBLISHING 2023
Copyright © Sana Twinkle 2023

All Rights Reserved.
ISBN: 978-93-56483-23-1

This book has been published with all reasonable efforts taken to make the material error-free after the consent of the author. No part of this book shall be used, reproduced in any manner whatsoever without written permission from the author, except in the case of brief quotations embodied in critical articles and reviews.

The Author of this book is solely responsible and liable for its content including but not limited to the views, representations, descriptions, statements, information, opinions and references ["Content"]. The Content of this book shall not constitute or be construed or deemed to reflect the opinion or expression of the Publisher or Editor. Neither the Publisher nor Editor endorse or approve the Content of this book or guarantee the reliability, accuracy or completeness of the Content published herein and do not make any representations or warranties of any kind, express or implied, including but not limited to the implied warranties of merchantability, fitness for a particular purpose. The Publisher and Editor shall not be liable whatsoever for any errors, omissions, whether such errors or omissions result from negligence, accident, or any other cause or claims for loss or damages of any kind, including without limitation, indirect or consequential loss or damage arising out of use, inability to use, or about the reliability, accuracy or sufficiency of the information contained in this book.

Author Biography

10-year-old Sana Twinkle is the author of this book. She is studying in BGS National Public School, in Bengaluru, India. She intended to create this book with her passion of putting her imagination in the form of poems, stories and travel blogs. With the support of her loving parents: Mr. Twinkle Mathew and Mrs. Aju joseph, and the help of her cute little sister, Evana Twinkle, 'The Unseen Showers' was born. All pictures in this book were hand drawn by Sana and Evana. Besides writing, other interests of Sana were: Art and craft, Dancing, Singing.

Thank you

*I heartfully give a thanks to all who helped me
throughout my life.
To my parents and grandparents for supporting me,
To my teachers for teaching me.
To my babysitters for helping me.
To my friends and cousins for entertaining me.
Special thanks to my sister who was by my side and
for drawing these pictures.
Everyone through these 10 years of my life,
Without them, this book will not stay alive.
This book is not just for me,
It is a credit for those surrounding me...*

Contents

1. When you are in..1
2. Pencil Shading..3
3. Losing a Friend..5
4. Why are you Here?..7
5. What AM I?...9
6. My dream school..11
7. Something that Made Me Twinkle 12
8. What She Does For Me 14
9. My Teachers 16
10. My First Crush 18
11. War 20
12. World Problems 22
13. The Strength of the Universe 25
14. Exams 27
15. Holi 29
16. Art 31
17. Spring 33
18. Death will be Sooner 35
19. Secrets 37
20. One Choice 39
21. Taking a Bath 41

22.	What Only An Eye Can See	43
23.	A Little Pinch of Salt	45
24.	Doctors	47
25.	Time	48
26.	Life	49
27.	When you Look at me	51
28.	Star Fish	53
29.	Shining Dew	55
30.	Silent Willows	57
31.	What I see in Velankanni	60
32.	Dubai Trip	62
33.	A Trip to Chennai	64
34.	My Kerala Trip	68
35.	A Trip to Goa	72
36.	A Trip to Jaipur, Agra, Delhi	75
37.	A Trip to Mysore	83
38.	The replica besides the real	86
39.	Independent life	88
40.	The Busy Bazaar	89
41.	The golden house	91
42.	Beauty all around us	92
43.	All the Little Minds	93
44.	My Letter to Protesters	95
45.	Mr. Ramatu and his Date Produce	97
46.	The Dark Room	99

Poems

WHEN YOU ARE IN...

When you are stuck inside a bush,

let free by cutting the branches.

When you find yourself falling from the sky,

open your invisible wings and fly.

When you are in a whale's mouth

Do not break yourself out and make it pout,

Tickle 'till he laughs and then get out.

When you are in the midst of a circle,

bond with all parts of it.

When a car is about to hit you,

go up to the footpath.

When the slingshot pulls you back,

tear the ropes with your bare hands.

When you do not know the way back home

wander deep,

in 'The Unseen Showers'...

PENCIL SHADING

Why only black,

with no other shade?

Why just makes you feel bland?

Not a drip of red,

nor a bit of blue,

all is just light and darkness.

But no, it is not as you think

it is full of color,

a color of story behind it.

You see pinks, blues, and yellows,

a long rainbow, just inside the black painting.

LOSING A FRIEND

A tree with a stump,

all its leaves wear off,

branches lose support.

All except one

stuck to a branch,

Losing a Friend

for more than decades.

As it weakens

and blown away by a gust of wind,

the stump feels what

its soul flying away,

leaving the body unmoved.

The last leaf of the tree

was its soul,

that barely could take.

Misery from clouds

as they break apart,

shed tears.

It gleams with the sunlight

as it falls onto,

the lonely stump.

And at that moment

for once in a lifetime,

there sprouts a little leaf!

WHY ARE YOU HERE?

To a mango given to the roadside beggars

He says, why are you here?

To the vines helping the old leaf

It says, why are you here?

To the glue filling the empty cracks of the pot

It says, why are you here?

To the teddy bear who puts the little girl to sleep

She says, why are you here?

To your mother who came to watch your talent show

You say, why are you here?

To your father who helps you carry the heavy baggage

You say, why are you here?

If you do all those then...

When you pray in the altar to God

He says, why are you here?

We all are here for a reason. Either to help you, or to protect you. There is no point in questioning that when you know the answer.

WHAT AM I?

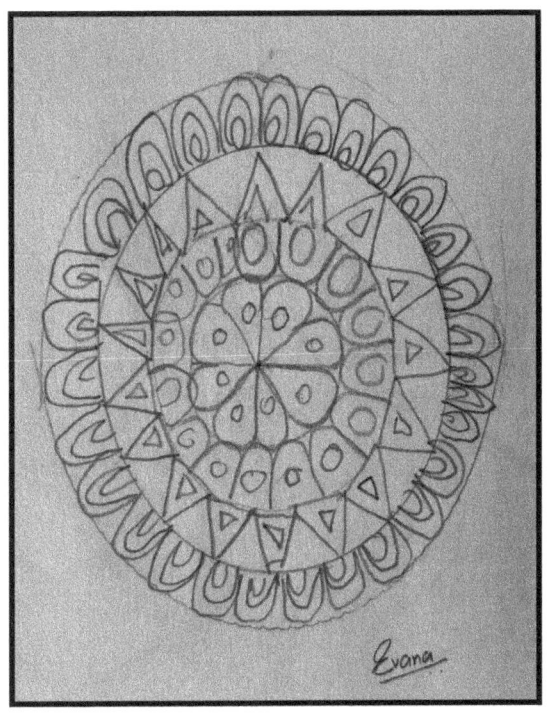

What am I, I ask myself

You are a dandelion!!

The birds and bees suck up your anger

And the wind blows your sadness away.

You are the sun

Lighting the world with your ideas

Making it a better place.

You are a cloud

You bring out rain drops to people

That send messages from heaven.

You are fire

That melts down the sad land of ice

Into a blooming paradise.

You are a tree

The strong roots of you save the world.

You are the mighty wind

Travel anywhere around.

You are the earth

A home for all of us!!

MY DREAM SCHOOL

My dream school is a school that welcomes all races and gives equality to all.

It is a school that takes the value of education to the jewels of the world and does not cost a penny..

It is a school that uses any method to turn the raw fruits ripe.

It is a school that casts out the ones who fade our smile and pull us back from the path of learning...

It is a school that finds and expresses our talent.

It is a school that never makes us feel alone.

This is the school I want to dwell in and others may do too.

SOMETHING THAT MADE ME TWINKLE

He being the first person I saw,

but I drove away from his hug.

He changed my stinky diapers up close,

when I just wanted to see him 50 feet away.

How hard of a journey of studying to become the top,

but he managed of only the hardest.

From me getting royalty, spoiling me rotten

I needed to pay by all my heart.

It is just like him giving me a huge palace

then, I burn it to ash.

It is just like him giving me a silver gown.

but all I did was throw it down.

He would give me the sun and the moon.

just for a bit of love from me.

I was born as a star in the sky,

but he made me twinkle.

WHAT SHE DOES FOR ME

My mom is the sweetest

she handles all the pressures I give her

And treats me to a pleasant smile.

She is like a reaching branch to the weeds

although they left it on purpose.

She is like the remaining colors of the rainbow to one

reaching out to it

although it slid back intentionally.

She suffers enough the condition I treat her in

but tries all her energy out to make me the best.

Oh Mother, you are unlike the rest!!

MY TEACHERS

Who formed a natural bond,

 with no hugs, kisses,

but with her books and knowledge.

They put up their energy,

the teachers, missing their family,

are loving enough to do whatever it takes.

All the algebra formulas,

to others, a pile of stress,

but to me, is a form of gifts.

There is this Tesla,

a car worth billion,

but a teacher is worth more than that.

The Buckingham Palace,

the home of Queen Elizabeth,

which is where I feel millions of them move in.

To see them leave, is normal for some,

but to me, it feels more painful than losing half my heart.

To many people, they are just teachers,

but to me, they are the multiverse.

I miss you so much Ma'am...

MY FIRST CRUSH

Something staying in me for a long, lasting time.

But letting it out would be like a humiliating rhyme.

I have a crush on the man, who practices his kindness

The one who gives every rag some riches.

I have a crush on the trees, not because of the green,

but the healthy fruits they share me to eat.

My First Crush

I have a crush on the doctors, taking their own beauty sleep

to the sick, he sows and reaps.

I have a crush on every little thing

From up the mountains to under the sea

the ozone layer, for taking in and out the harm,

the decomposers, for cleaning our land.

the teachers, for believing in me,

and those who encourage me.

My family, for being with me
and the earth, for giving life to me.

But most of all,
I have a crush on me, for being me.

WAR

On horses and elephants

behind lies guns and swords,

I think, why did they do this.

All stay the same,

either the life of the people,

or the stay of our nation.

From these billions of years,

things have changed,

but what stayed was war.

They could construct new satellites,

find new experiments,

and flourish their province in the time they pack for war.

I think, why do they risk it.

All till' today

if not, they waste the time in war,

they would have made tomorrow a better place.

This is what I want to change

WORLD PROBLEMS

All in one, one in all

1000 cultures in every country,

north to south, east to west

but is it certainly not the best.

Why block the girls from freedom?

why not make them navigate to space,

take some pictures of the James Webb

explain theories about them,

other than make them sit around

waiting for their "charming prince".

Why drop out of your knowledge?

change our ideology,

to do something surreal

be a part of the terrorists,

and threaten the globe.

Why differentiate two people?

if you cannot do that with pillows,

all the population are meant to follow their dreams

and not only those of your choosing.

Why not look at the dark sides of your streets?

the ones sleeping there,

we do not know where we land on at birth

and make it look like we chose that life.

Why sit and relax?

when you see problems all round

with us playing 24-7,

then scatter around at the realizing moment.

The world is a good place

but not the perfect one,

there should come up theories

and leave barren all the silliness,

as all of us newborns are on a mission

to make the world better.

THE STRENGTH OF THE UNIVERSE

All those women, young and old,

all have a heart of gold.

We see batman, superman, and hulk,

but women have powers that they do not have.

They know how to make a copy of themselves,

but those of who are young and eyed to the universe.

They are the only ones,

who hold the title of the graceful swan.

With their twirls and leaps in spotlight,

seeing their clear and fragile body,

and graceful smile bonding.

They are the real strength,

who escaped the men who pulled them back,

and fought them to the finish line.

They are called the real competitors,

with skill, grace and will against their opponents.

This is the day,

that looks up on us women as the best.

EXAMS

My soul crying through these heaps of books

As my brain dies out of battery.

The puddle of sweat and nerve on my notes

because of my face boiling with stress.

Thousands of times the chapter read

still nothing on my head.

This is when all vacations planned for summer

leave a huge trail of misery.

Should I have heard my parents

that I have studied earlier.

Should I have not been busy playing

and listen to the teacher.

I should have taken all this advise

and would not be in despair.

Now the thing I do is hang my head.

With all my happy days ended

because of this stroke of regret.

HOLI

Today is a special festival

where even Miss world loves ruining her beauty.

With all of us dressed in vivid bombs of color

rainbows do not need the gloomy rain anymore.

The day no one cares about the boss' new suit

and is brave to fill it with tons of stains.

Where our caste system has collapsed

with everyone looking the same.

No one makes any arguments

as they are busy in fun.

Who wants to listen to the teacher

and wear a clean uniform.

This day, even she will not mind.

Then is the only time our parents let us play in the mud

And they will also too.

ART

A bunch of colors, a bunch of paints

can turn a canvas into a wonderland.

A bunch of papers and a bit of glue

can turn materials into a character.

All you need is your imagination

to fly high and abroad.

Art

All you need is your imagination

to create something new.

With a bunch of wires

a robot we can make.

With a bunch of clay

a sculpture we can make.

With a computer

an app we can make.

With a bunch of bricks

a house we can make.

With a bunch of seeds

a forest we can make.

With a piece of land

a country we can make.

And with a bunch of humans

a generation we can make.

This is called art.

SPRING

There melts the cold

giving the look of warmth,

This hail going on for months

softened into a chill breeze.

All this anger

all this pain,

all this pressure and these sufferings,

melted as the snow in our hearts.

All comes to chill as we think of the birds flying back,

when the trees dress up,

and blossoms rise,

The river flows slowly...

Not as might as monsoon,

sitting under the shade with the glam of sun,

all is chill...

DEATH WILL BE SOONER

As you blow off your fiery dreams into a pile of ashes

As you leave the river of time to flow barely

As you let a flower to wither

You will realize, Death will be sooner

As you separate the leaves who are paired inseparable

As you hid one of the bundled matchsticks

As you neglect a broken egg

You will realize, Death will be sooner

As you scare away a tortoise that made you trip

As you ignore the bees who speaks up to you

As you are determined to be compared with the butterflies

You will realize, Death will be sooner

As you make yourself a heavy rainfall

As you question the flowers for blooming

As you fear the lion's hunger at one glimpse

You will realize, Death will be sooner

SECRETS

What is safely locked in a cage in my head

unwilling to escape.

It is either kept quiet about

or replaced with another.

Those shining stars come down as I do

but some throw me back.

The splashy waves washing the fear out of me

but some take me with them.

The sprouts grow me out of them

or grow to see me small.

The never was it known what happens

right now, or at the future.

But whatever comes through, it stays a secret.

ONE CHOICE

Whether to rule as united or divided

you have only one choice.

To think of you being a successful,

or hide as a failure

you only have one choice.

Whether you will give your whole bag to those unprivileged

or to take them as your needs,

you have only one choice.

Whether to stay home in your baggy pants

or walk around your globe,

you only have one choice.

Whether to sit under the stump of a tree

or play around your circle,

you have only one choice.

Whether to follow your herd

or to build a house on Mars,

One Choice

you only have one choice.

Whether to climb up the Mount Everest

or to give up by seeing its height,

you only have one choice.

Whether to enjoy all you have quickly

or to sit around until your final breath,

you only have one choice.

Whether to continue it or end it,

you only have one choice.

TAKING A BATH

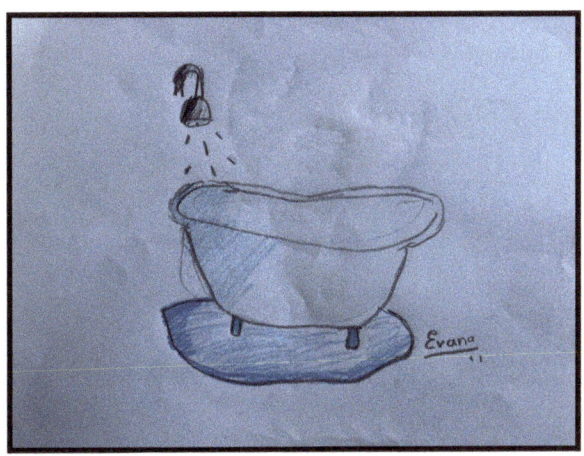

We all take a bath every day,

to remove all our germs.

the germs that break all the eggs out of the carton.

the germs that divide the reds and blues,

and all bad omen,

all collected,

with the foam bubbles of soap.

Taking a Bath

After that waterfall from the shower gives you a rinse.

Those who anger that get eternal peace,

Those in misery that feel a lot comfortable,

Those selfish come down to earth,

All the hunger and thirst shall be satisfied,

and all earthlings,

feel that everything in the past vanished

and new clothes are put on.

WHAT ONLY AN EYE CAN SEE

My eyes are not only my home of sight

They are the link to the world.

The narrow path leading a warm lake

Lies a bird, who glances at the first sight

Of heaven.

Who found a faded carnation on their journey

The sunlight gave a glimmer facing

The only tunnel to the homely lake

In a tiny dot invisible from the world outside.

I stood there corpse

With my soul amplifying from the feeling

Of hearts of either a bird

Or a butterfly.

It gave me the wings of a butterfly

And the song of the bird.

Where i appeared on the hands of the waves

Where the sun shone on a golden amethyst

With the quartz of a gram of happiness

Which only a deeper look of our sight

Can see.

Moral

The wings of the butterfly, the song of the bird, the beauty of the amethyst and the gram of happiness all lies in the talent of the eyes where the pupil does not matter on the color , but on the talent and the most interesting things what an eye can see which are the elements of the beautiful world of sight

A LITTLE PINCH OF SALT

A little pinch of salt

Can turn into a city.

Just like how a little work of hand

can give you a patent.

Everything little we see

around and about us

can reach the sky in its own way.

How this little seed lying on a shade

can grow a whole forest

without my helping hand.

And seeing

a little child we call us

going hand in hand as slaves of earth

And bringing in new boons to our descendants...

DOCTORS

My dream is to become a doctor

but not a doctor who cures only your health problems.

I will cure the ones who hide behind a corner

I will cure the ones who sit there and cry.

The ones who thought they had no butterfly wings,

The ones who are called a broken vase sold,

The ones who think kicking them is common,

The ones who feel like a mango being eaten,

I'm the one who wants to cure the problems of the world

where everyone from everywhere can come to me,

and I cure their problem.

Those are the real doctors

TIME

Drops of water go down the drain every second,

unwilling to wait for the further ones.

When you are going to get your keys as you settle you dog to walk,

it mercilessly runs to chase a blue butterfly.

As you take the pretty pink lily for your vase,

it loses its shape when you reach.

Now you look at the brightness the sun gives you,

the next minute is a dim of it.

The last note saved for later,

becomes a pile of notes doing now.

Every minute is spent doing good,

as who knows what happens in the next.

LIFE

Life of yours is a river

Flowing down calmly.

The river moves aside from the trash

Or anything that raises the waves.

It gently flows with a mind of peace

Getting the air, the trees sway.

Never worried about the end

But is collected the rain of passion

That comes from the clouds.

Boats with not a single person

But positivity flying about.

It flows slowly

At winters water bodies struggle

But this one flow.

With none of bond with negativity

Only with the bond of peace.

Slowly the river is freezing

But it still moves with its happiness.

Alas, the river froze

But its sign of positivity never did.

Moral

Always fill your life with positivity so if your life ends, the positivity does not and is shared to all the beings of the world so we can live at least in our positivity

WHEN YOU LOOK AT ME

When you look at me

You will look at the rainfall

When I look at you

I can hear the raindrops

The wind is blowing

blowing your own mind

And when I write the lines

the lines of this song

As you can see the waterfall

Minimizing as rain

And I will never forget your heart beat...!

STAR FISH

Inside-Outside

Where the amethyst turns gold

With scales of stardust,

Which was crystal clear

The reflection of your smile

That shines so bright,

It was the end of the day, the start of the night

The star's reflection oh so bright

It rises so you can reach it,

The start of tomorrow's boon

Reflecting the sun

Gives you the day

A lot of fun.

Moral

Make today fun

SHINING DEW

It shines as it echoes:

As clear as a crystal

When I saw it, it reminded me something

Something I never knew inside my heart

Filled up a pool, with tears of joy

It rises and rises

Where I can feel it

It was neither salty nor sweet

It filled up the pool that was about to overflow

it turned invisible that felt the heat in my palms

It rose to a little cloud

And became a little friend

At that time, I realized

I had to share my joy

But the time I was surprised

The joy shared itself

It poured into the world

Fills more pools

and shares the joy

SILENT WILLOWS

Silent willows hanging in the cool breeze

Reminds me when I bathe in the dead sea

The willows that is blessed among the wings of the dragonflies

Where now is invisible, but visible in my heart

It floats like a feather, flies like a bird

Above my head, touching the coral tip

Which surrounds me like a flower garden

I do not love you where you are in a droop

The dead sea starts to die

And black in my eye

Oh, my dear, please hear me cry

I cannot see the world, all black and white

But a tear fell in the dead sea

It grew and it grew

Reaching me as I laid on the soft melt of my heart

And it took me

To the past

Where i bathe

In the dead sea

Near the silent willows

Hanging in the cool breeze

MORAL

Your life is a book, you can take your life to a happy memory when facing a sad time

Travel Blogs

WHAT I SEE IN VELANKANNI

A place in Tamil Nadu, known for being a pilgrim center,

But I see many kids selling things all day,

People eating and sleeping in the streets,

The paralyzed weakly trying their best to survive,

Many asking for food and money.

Why can't we create more schools,

So, the laboring younglings have a second home to learn.

Why can't we create more homes,

So, we won't suffer the hard rock pillows of the streets.

Why can't we create more hospitals,

So, we will not see the paralyzed struggling any longer.

Why can't we create more jobs,

So, we all have enough for a comfortable life.

If many are praying for the good life,

Why can't we give it to them.

If many are suffering back there,

Why can't we comfort them.

Will it be more worth in a pilgrimage center?

DUBAI TRIP

We have gone up in the sky

to birds and Dubai, we say hi.

Swift in the Marina Cruise

With a hearty dinner and shows, we amuse.

Things so ancient and beautiful

It looked Mural but colorful

but this classical Emirati house

now is deserted like a place for mouse.

Shopping Sprees and lots to do

Dubai Mall, we have come for you

Coming up to the Burj Khalifa

In the 124th floor, how cool the area

Dancing like a ballerina

A breathtaking water arena

A photo frame that frames Dubai

You can put your photo for UAE to say hi

The place full of fast rides and fun

In all, Ferrari world is number one

From a desert to reaching the sky

but there is still an end and we have to say goodbye

GOODBYE DUBAI!!

A TRIP TO CHENNAI

Before the trip

8/9/2021 Wednesday, 11:50 AM

I was in online school quickly completing my work so none of my work will be due when I come back, I informed the leave letter to my teacher asking for permission. My teacher accepted my request and told me to quickly show my notebook before I go. I changed into some comfortable clothes and cut off all contact with friends. I left my online session and I had put my laptop on shutdown. My father then packed my laptop and all device chargers, removed the network connections and we prayed for a good trip. I informed the leave letter to all my co-circular classes and left our home. We went to the basement and then went inside the car. We went out if our home and crossed the toll gate to leave the border of Bengaluru, Karnataka.

1:30 PM

We reached the border of Tamil Nadu and passed a few stops for required breaks, we stopped at a hotel to eat some snacks and then went on our journey. We crossed Kanchipuram, the district of sarees. They are very common there since a lot of people grow silk and weave sarees out of them.

We crossed another hotel for a coffee break. There, they served filter coffee. A traditional meal.

7:00 PM

After many hours of boredom, we finally reached our hotel. Our hotel's name was Savera and it was rated 4 stars, we parked our car and then brought all the luggage. My father then checked in our hotel and signed a few papers. We then got our hotel key that was a card to swipe in the slot. Our room was room 921 in the 9th floor. And that was the start of our trip.

During the trip

9/9/2021 Thursday, 7:00 AM
The start of our Chennai trip, how refreshing!

Opening my eyes to the beautiful city life of Chennai, The colorful capital of Tamil Nadu.

We went to the Hotel Restaurant and ate Ghee Roast and the yummiest of pasta.

I took a walk with my mother and saw a big oven at the right, pots colored in the Indian tricolor at the front , a wall design with plates on the left, a big piano at the back and so much more!

10:30 AM

I went to the USA consulate to renew my passport. They checked my FedEx DD and our passports. We then went to another building where we were given a token number that was 20, and was then asked to sit in the waiting room until my token number was called. When it was called, we went into a room where a person asked for my name, my passport, and my FedEx DD. We then sat again in the waiting room for a long time. There were 2 world maps, one of USA and one of the worlds. The world map attracted me and I started teaching my sister about the world. A boy listened and then went into the breastfeeding room. My sister followed him and there she hid. The boy introduced himself there and then we played hide and seek. The boy left when we were about to play knock-knock and then our token was called again. We went into the same room and then there was an American interviewer that gave us an interview. We then left the building and went to our hotel in an auto.

2:30 PM

I went to the Loyola college where my mother's friend Anita aunty was. She was an English professor there. They were big groups of colleges that were of computer science, social studies and much more.

There was a big church surrounded with birds and geese, we prayed for some time in the church and then went out, I was very thirsty so we went into the school cafeteria and ate and drank. I ate chocolate doughnut and drank Sweet Lime juice. We then left the college.

4:00 PM

We went to Muthu aunt's home where many years ago, she took care of my mother when my father was in America. Achu aunty who had a son, he was 7 years old. We gave him a science kit that we played with. We made a volcano and then left

7:00 PM

We went to the largest beach in India, The Marina Beach that has a lot of seashore that was filled with shops, we stood there for some time and then ate dinner. And that was the end of Day 1

10/9/2021 Friday, 12:00 PM

We went to the science city where they showed science by physics and fun, I learned about the lemmeck that can heal influenza, cough and cold and is native place is New Guinea and so much more, we saw a 5D movie and I felt like I was flying in the sky, we had a great time.

The end of the trip

11/9/2021 Saturday, 7:00 AM

The Morning of the end of our trip has started, I have one last glimpse of the colorful capital of Tamil Nadu, The pots with the Indian Tricolor, the design with plates and much more, I say bye to what interesting memories Chennai has given me to my future self. There is 5 more years till I come here again. Until then bye Chennai.

MY KERALA TRIP

I had a very fun trip in Kerala. The southernmost of our diverse nation. Nature breathtaking to see. The freshest natural air gusting over us that breathes me back to life. Home to cultural delicacies such as Rambutan. But the most important events are just to see my loving grandparents and to celebrate my Holy Communion.

We came on April 30th to Athirampuzha all the way from Bangalore, Karnataka. I saw happiness at first sight seeing my grandparents as I ran inside the house. It was very huge compared to my tiny apartment in Bangalore. The Backyard was very big and full of various plants. We could play all kinds of games such as Frisbee. Me and my sisters always chit-chat as we dine together, sit together, and sleep together

Today was May 1st, 2022

We took my cousin to my other grandparents' house. I rushed to them happily. There was a Smart Television where we watched YouTube and Netflix. In the backyard, there was a swing that I loved the most. A ride in our minds named Crazy Ride was applied on the swing. It was made to make us feel dizzy and to make us have fun at the same time. We also watched our two favorite channels that are Windows Vista and Country Balls. We also made new friends that are Jemima and Sharon. We do a lot of drawings made entirely out of nature. We stayed there for about a week

Starting from May 2nd, I had classes for my holy communion in St. Mary's Forane Church. In my first day I was a bit shy. They made me learn a lot of prayers. There, I made my first friend named Hannah and my second friend that was Angel and many more. Hannah, Anna Maria, and the teachers helped me to understand what they were saying. In class Intermission, me and my friends walk towards places around the church and chit-chat together.

The 6th of May was a bit painful. I needed to take surgery in my leg to remove a needle stuck inside. We first took an X-ray of it and to my horror, the needle was very big. We then had lunch at F8's and went to a surgeon. Then I went to the treatment room. 10 seconds before all the pain. They put a syringe through my leg and removed it. Then my leg was stitched up and filled with cotton. I could not walk for 3 days and needed to take rest

In May 7th, I was on floating land with the pension squad. Meeting and greeting so many new friends was a great moment to learn new things during my summer vacation. I learned a new game called Little Rose Flower that was a local game in Kerela. We also sang songs and danced to music. It was fun

In May 10th, I went to my cousin Isabel's house with all my cousins. It had a lot of nature surrounding me. We walked on top of a log as a balance beam and crossed it. We also ate ice cream and saw a man catching fish from a deep lake with a fishing net. We even went on a boat that was bobbing up and down.

On the day after that. My cousin Malha came to my house for a sleepover. We played a game called 7 continents, ate pizza, and did a night drawing competition and a long night chat. It was so fun with all of us together. As the more the marrier, the greater the trip will be.

13th of May was my confession date. I put all my sins on a paper and was on the confession line. When it was my turn, I told my sins to a father and he gave me a penance. I left the confession table like an angel

14th of May was the main event. I received my first holy communion at St. Mary's. I stopped by my house to take many photos and headed to EXCALIBUR. I got many gifts and did a few performances. It was the happiest moment of my life

On the day after that we went to Play World with Ashlyn, Ashton, Ethan, Malha, Isabel, Evana, and me. My favorite place was the trampoline and the big slide. We were there for about 2 hours and we ate ice cream with everyone. I had the most awesome time there.

On 18th of May was my Mother's Birthday. I was so excited to show her my gifts. I hid them in an online treasure hunt to make it fun to find them. We cut a coffee cake and we went to our other cousins' house to celebrate

On 21st of May, we went to Mallapally. We took a stop at Nallumanikaatu with the fresh wind and fresh snacks at 4 pm. At Mallapally, there was so much nature around us. We met new friends called Kris and Keith living in the neighboring house. We ate very naturally prepared food and played Red Light, Green Light. It was so fun.

On 27th of May, we went to my grandfather's old church built in 1st Century AD. That was where Mother Mary came to give food to hungry shepherd kids. We also went to my grandfather's brother's house and met his friend in school. It was awesome to see these historic places. And that was the end of our trip. The thing that I love the most about this trip was the fact I made a lot of memories and enjoying my childhood. As I write the words in this travelogue, I relive this precious time in my life!!!

A TRIP TO GOA

Our loving grandparents, who knew we love to see

The world with all blue and green

They took us to where

lies a touch of both Indian and Portuguese

Goa is the place

They're seen those beautiful churches

The Basilica of Bom Jesus

All in Old goa

which bring back the old, holy taste

There lie the Agoda fort of the courageous

who hunt for us weaklings

With all these shattered down

Like the beautiful St. Augustine tower

which is now all in ruins

Our architecture, for them is now history

The heart of their jets at the Naval Aviation Museum

"Where every landing is mandatory, not the takeoff"

and Car war

Where the ships set sail towards the future

preserved in popular museums

But all rain has a rainbow at the end of it

In the new goa, the new land we see

The paradise of it

Which is none without the Donar Pola

Who stands at the heart of beautiful beaches

the mix of white and clear blue

The Calangute, Palolem, Candolim, Colva and Anjuna

in the touch of the beautiful sunrise

overlooking its horizon

Much deeper, jumps playful dolphins

Along our dolphin watch

swimming along with our boats.

But the real golden pot of treasure at the end of it

Was the pleasant journey to and from

and every moment with my family.

A TRIP TO JAIPUR, AGRA, DELHI

Long ago, there led a piece of land where all flourished, it was such a wealthy nation with fine goods. Many other provinces wanted to trade goods with it. But the plan hiding inside them was that they will soon control the nation and loot all their riches.

Now, I had come to see the historical triangle that holds many ruins awaiting, as their riches are now ancient history.

JAIPUR (RAJASTHAN)

Jaipur, the pink city, which is surprisingly not pink! It is actually a brick-like color. Prince Albert nicknamed it as 'The pink city' and the name stuck.

We first went to visit the **Hawa Mahal**. Built by Maharaja Pratap Singh. It was known as the Palace of air. It was given the name as it overlooks hundreds of tiny windows bringing in fresh, cool air. It was a huge 5-storey building used to worship Lord Krishna as it holds his beautiful crown at the topmost floor. So, if you are feeling hot after a busy day in Jaipur, come here to cool off with nature as your fan.

Next, we went to the **Jantar Mantar.** Built by Maharaja Jai Singh. There is where the calculations started before it really started. In our modern days, we use wires, electricity, mechanics, and internet to perform calculations. But the calculations were done here without even the concept of them. Here, we can find the local time, latitude, longitude, altitude, horoscope etc. with simple structures, all working in solar power. How intelligent were the kings who made this, showing all future technology in the past. Same available in Delhi.

The **city palace** was where we went next. Built by Maharaja Jai Singh. Beholding the appliances of the royal family, which now stands as exhibits there. The throne, where they sit, solid gold and beautifully carved. Every utensil they use was made with precious stones. And their beautiful clothes were made with the finest of the materials. The exquisite goods made their gowns large and heavy that the queens need wheelchairs to move around. That was just as valuable as the throne. Not even a single thing is ordinary in this extraordinary palace.

After, we went to **Amber fort,** The fort of Maharaja Man Singh. it has a huge number of crooked steps, tough to climb. Here, we see the disadvantages of Raja Man Singh's wives, the queens. He made one small apartment for each of his 12 wives, and the only place they can meet is the hall between the apartments. No queen can go to each other's flat and all they do is under supervision. We are lucky enough to go to our friends' houses without arms or a camera above.

Then, we went to the **Jaigarh fort.** Ruled by Man Singh. The fort used to track down their nemesis. There lies holes in each wall pointing downwards. That is where they throw down hot water and hot oil to burn them. They showcase the world's largest cannon here.

We rushed off to **Nahargarh fort.** Built by Maharaja Sawai Jai Singh. Here, we see the sunset view of the bustling capital of Rajasthan. Seeing the sun shoot up its rays while it dissolves in the clouds overlooking a whole city from an ancient fort is a beautiful combination seen in paintings. This is a view you cannot miss.

We then looked at the water view of the **Jal Mahal**. An underwater palace of Maharaja Jai Singh. It is a 5-storey building where 4 of them are submerged. Unlike all lakes we often see, this one is clear and pure.

The night is the best timing to see **Choki Dhani .** It gives us local Rajasthani cuisine for dinner and a lot of activities you can see only locally. The cost here is very cheap and the people here show kindness is by greeting with a 'Ram Ram Sa'.

The next day, we went to **Kanak Vrindavan.** It shows us a Mandir in the heart of a beautiful garden. with lush green trees and hot pink posies. The pearl color of the temple makes it stand out.

Then, we went to the **Albert Hall Museum.** Showing us the handicrafts of the people back then. From the beautiful pottery to the large carpets and chandeliers. From the beautiful sculptures to the marvelous architecture. It has it all.

AGRA (UTTAR PRADESH)

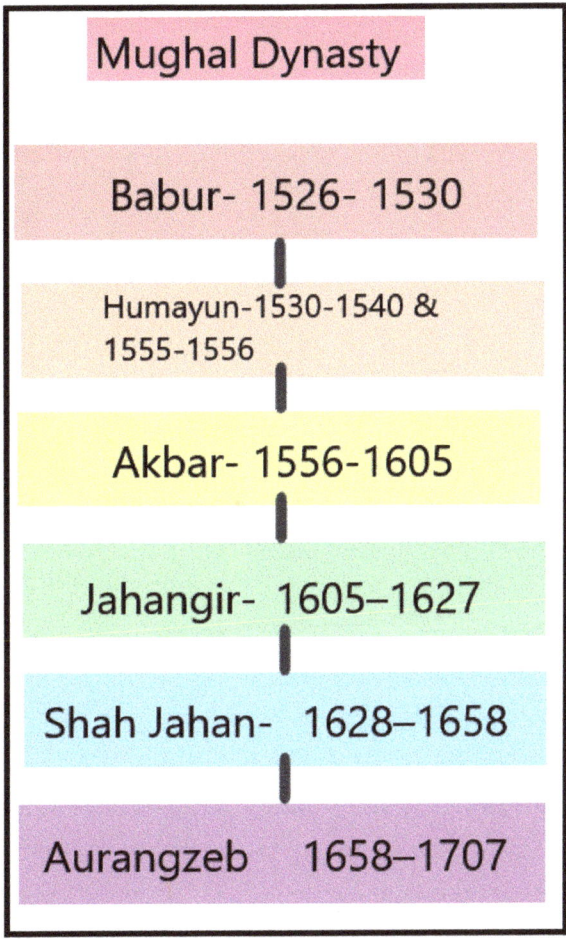

We went to **Fatehpur Sikri.** It was where the Mughal emperor Akbar and his 3 wives lived. In Fatehpur, there is a mosque, made with red sandstone with the designs of 3 religious places: A Muslim Mosque, a Hindu temple and a Christian church. This diversity resembles his 3 wives in favor of their religion (Ruqaiya Sultan, Jodhaa, Mariam) . Here is also where he started a new religion in the mix of these 3 ones (Din-I-llahi). Sikri is where they live. That was acres of land all to themselves. The rooms were filled with luxury, gold and silver, valuable material. Which is now looted by the British. leaving behind red sandstone. Some of the places there are Jodhaa

Mahal, Birbal mahal (built for his favorite minister), Akbar's bedroom, Ruqaiya's dressing table, Akbar's rose-water bath etc.

Next, was a very important one. The **Taj Mahal.** One of the 7 wonders of the world. Its surface filled with pure white marble, with the beautiful inlay art, shining like the full moon at night. Every little detail has an expensive cost behind it. It was built by Shah Jahan. Mumtaz, his favorite wife was buried at its heart. It is symmetrical at all sides. At its opposite, lies the Black Taj. Made to be the shadow of the real Taj. But he only completed the foundation before he was house-arrested. His soul was then buried next to his wife at the Taj.

The next day, we saw the **Agra Fort.** The fort that took 4 generations to complete (Akbar, Jahangir, Shah Jahan, Aurangzeb). It was filled with various protections to prohibit the enemies from entering. These are done with a ton of intelligence built in and took a lot of effort to make. Akbar and Jahangir preferred red sandstone whereas Shah Jahan changed it to white marble. Each of the palaces have 2 courts, Diwan- I- Khas (The meeting area for the VIP's) and Diwan-I-Aam (The meeting area for the commoners). Shah Jahan's daughters did not get a husband made for them. As they were waiting to go on a chariot for once in a lifetime. He built them chariot-shaped bedrooms so that they can stay in it 24/7.

Then, we saw the **Baby Taj.** This was built for the family of Jahangir's wife, Nur Jahan. Made before the actual Taj. As he was drunk, his wife took over the kingdom. This had the same details as the Taj which is certainly more beautiful than its baby version.

DELHI

Then, we went to the **Akshardham Mandir,** a very holy and peaceful place. Once we enter, we feel a sudden stoke of goodness from the ten directions. On every pillar you see, stands handicraft idols circling it. They also make us follow the path of its founder, Bhagwan Swaminarayan.

The next day lands the visit to **Humayun's tomb.** Built by his wife. The reason for his death is that when he wanted to look at the stars, he slipped off and died. It stands on top of Isa Khan's Garden, and at the opposite side of Isa Khan's tomb. Who died before Humayun. They both were warring kings buried in the same place. There, them, and their family members were buried together.

Next, we went to **Agrasen ki Baoli.** It is a large stepwell that was used in the olden days to collect water. Now, this stands as a tourist attraction and photo destination.

Next, we went to the **Red Fort.** Built by Shah Jahan **This** already seems familiar to you as this is where every flag is hoisted in Independence day, and where the march past ends in Republic Day. Surrounding this, is a city called Shah-Jahan-Abad which is now known as Old Delhi. It has a whole market for the royal family and holds a whole town for the VIP's. To be honest, their bathroom is bigger than our bungalow in my native.

Then, we went to the **Chandni Chowk.** That used to be known as the bazaar for the commoners. It was so crowded that our ribs almost got squeezed. A ton of people begged for money and forced us to buy their products. I cannot help it but that is how busy bazaars are like.

In the evening, we visited the **India Gate.** The gateway towards our country, hearted at the capital. When we pass through it, we see how much our country is struggling 'till now. Tons of soldiers gave up their blood for Mother India and her protection. We remember the immortal acts of these people after seeing the **War Memorial.**

Next, we saw the **Raj Ghat.** The divine place where the father of our nation, Mahatma Gandhi Ji was buried. But, instead of mourning his death, we feel proud to have someone like him, who fought all his life until his last breath. We must stay inspired by him and create more Gandhis like him.

Then, we went to the **Rastrapati Bhavan.** The house of the Honorable President. Right next to the **Parliament.** This is how much of a building is needed to keep our country on going. Without it, we would not be able to stand without anyone controlling us...

Next day, we went to the **Indira Gandhi Museum.** It shows the history and livelihood of the first woman prime minister. It shows us that she loves to spend most of her time at her study, reading books and newspapers. But most of all, she is full of simplicity. So simple that the dress worn in her marriage was a second-hand sari made by her father.

Then, we went to the **Pradhan Mantri Sangrahalaya.** This shows us the history, timeline, and interesting moments in the life of prime ministers. From the ones who contributed in fighting against the British to the ones managing our country recently.

Next, was the **Lotus Temple.** India's national flower, surrounded by the clear waters and greenery. The park surrounding it became a local picnic spot, tourist attraction and most importantly, a mandir of worship.

Last, lies the **Qutub Minar.** Made by Qutbuddin Aibak, founder of the Slave Dynasty. His granddaughter, Razia Begum, is the first empress of India. It is a mosque made after the destruction of 28 temples. It shows the findings made in India before it reached the globe. The Europeans found various technologies, but little did they know that they were found in India before. The Qutub Minar is a good example of that.

The Riches are now looted, converted into ruins. These stories of rich kings and queens are now your history portion.

A TRIP TO MYSORE

Mysore, the greenery and lively people here in Karnataka, the total opposite of Bengaluru (where I live). This lush green area also hides behind some attractions and history. I will now show them to you.

We first went on the top of a hill, The **Chamundeshwari Temple** seated at the Chamundi hills. This was a great experience for me as this was the first temple I have been to in the birthplace of Hinduism. This was where Mysore got its current name. It was believed that an evil demon king named Mahishasura was killed by the goddess Durga here. As it was a great miracle, the people decided to name this place after the incident. 'Mahishooru'. The British simplified it to Mysore and it was later known as Mysuru.

Located in the center of Mysore, there stands the royal and famous **Mysore Palace**. It used to be the palace of the Wadiyar Dynasty and the seat of the Kingdom of Mysore. Legend says that the royal family still lives here. We can find the Chamundi temple as we look eastwards. This is known as the City of Palaces and has 7 palaces at its foot including this one. And, just like other palaces, luxury is everywhere.

We ate our lunch like a princess. Seated in royal chairs with the palace architecture all around us. The **Lalitha Mahal**. Where we get to stay a night or 2 in the life of royalty. You have the royal tub of the king as your swimming pool. The queen's ballroom as your party hall and the garden of the royal family is all yours.

Next, we went to the **Railway Museum**. Here is where we can see what was before the public transportation we use today. We also get to ride on a model toy train and eat in a train-like cafeteria.

Then, we went to the **St. Philomena Church.** The building was named after a saint named St. Philomena. It was very tall, about the height of a skyscraper. It was filled with beautiful German architecture everywhere you go.

We went to **Srirangapatna** to look at the tomb of Tipu Sultan. It is now a local and well-known pilgrimage spot. Buried in this Gumbaz is the Tipu sultan and his family.

Last, we went to the beautiful **Brindavan Gardens.** It is a symmetrical garden that makes it easy to get lost in the beauty of this garden. Surrounding this home of nature, there lie dancing fountains, looking like dancing ballerinas down the porch. At the end of the day, the fountains show us a memorable performance.

There was so much to see in only a day at Mysore, imagine if I would stay here for a week or a month.

Stories

THE REPLICA BESIDES THE REAL

Laila was a self-trained dancer from India. She was so good that she won many awards and shortlists, and was even appointed as ‹The graceful dancer› by the count. She became famous by playing her beats at important events. The next event around the corner was ‹Dancers Day' auditions. They were the auditions to select a dancer to represent the province in Dancers Day, competing across many. Laila accepted her challenge and worked 24/7.

Meanwhile, there lived a toymaker who got a lot of pay, but was never happy with it. He was greedy and jealous of Laila, as she would totally represent the country and wow the crowd. Then, he thought of a plan.

He worked hours, turning into days. Until he made his final product, 5 beautiful dolls that dance better than the graceful dancer. He then ran to the count to show him his project.

He first thought it was a joke, but his jaw dropped to see that it was real. 5 dolls beat the graceful dancer. He immediately called Laila saying that her role was given to the dolls. She sat there devastated. But she wanted to go to the competition and learn a few tricks from them.

The audition day arrived. there stood the whole state beholding the 5 dolls up stage. Their gorge look got everyone clicking their shutters. But, as the song played, one doll was too fast for the beat, one was too slow for it, one was crashing the other which fell, and the 5th doll remained as a statue. All the earlier cheers fell out.

Laila could not help but run on stage and show how it is done. She danced like her title, leaving the audience in awe within every move. Cheers were on the tables again.

The toymaker was fooled, but also learnt a valuable lesson.

"Even a statue of gold cannot replace the real man"

INDEPENDENT LIFE

There are trees home to mother birds, they collect their food from the ground and give it to their babies. Now, they are old enough to learn how to fly. But they still depended on their parents for food. Slowly, their wings and bodies grew so much that now even the mothers start complaining. But they were so stubborn that they refused. Then, the mother bird had a plan. She sat upon a tree branch with no work. when the birds cried for food, she did not move. This went for days until they were so angry that they jumped down to find food themselves. They flew and fell until they finally learned how to fly. The mother bird was happy that her plan was a success

We all should be independent and do our own work. We are never to be stubborn to those who help us. We should thank them for their hard work.

THE BUSY BAZAAR

Me and my brother took a walk around a huge place

It was busy, but not an office

It was big, but not a skyscraper

Was for shopping, but not a mall

Serves great cuisine, but not a restaurant

Shows our country, but not a map

It was nothing but the BUSY BAZAAR

In the first stall, we see a bhai making Kashmiri tea

Some of us call it cashmere tea, but it is just like the name

We see a woman making brooms with weeds and dry grass

It was very creative, also helps to save the environment

Can also be a good thing for my mom to make from our farm produce

and help others around the world

We then saw another bhai

He was stuffing toys

My brother puffed the plush up with cotton

Now it looks like it is a foodie

A bhai selling dessert

all like the soft cotton

melts in your mouth

with the same, smooth taste

A lot of busy things, but at the end there is a fun park

but it is not with carousels and roller coasters

But horse riding, henna applying

Kabaddi matches and more desi games

THE GOLDEN HOUSE

Our final exams are over, summer has started. We all discuss on where we will go for our vacation. My family does not have enough money as the others. But we will make sure that we can go somewhere special.

A few days of planning later, we decided to go to Tamil Nadu. We failed finding cheap hotels until we came upon a guest house. They were called, "House of gold" although it did not look like gold at all.

We opened the doors of the quarter and were heartly welcomed. We did not mind their small room, otherwise they treated us like royalty. They offered to cook for us, clean for us and didn't even mind when we asked them to clean after Chinni (the family dog) pooped on the tiles.

The most heart-touching moment was when they told us to sleep in their single bed and they slept on the floor.

In our leaving day, especially, they helped us a lot. They booked our transport, helped pack our things and instead of us paying them, they gave us money.

These people have hearts of gold, filling their guesthouse with all that love. I think that is why it is called "House of gold"

I was mistaken. the gold was in the inside of the house, not the outside

BEAUTY ALL AROUND US

In our city, most of us slaughter animals and eat them, The same thing in grandma's place. In which we were about to go for our uncle's wedding. The parties there do not happen in banquet halls or tents, the happen out in the open forests. We were about to cook some chicken for the wedding before a close call came that all the guests were vegetarians.

The wedding then started, those come from here and there. Until all those invited came. All, except the musician. This was a disgrace to our tradition. And even worse, Uncle love music so much that if there is no music in a party then there is no use. We were about to lose hope when something magical happened.

There opens the curtains, The birds sing a melodious chirp on the tree branch that meditates everyone.

He sings in tune of the rooster's loud cry. Pigs oink there beat to amuse the overlooking crowd. Monkeys blast the stage by showing us an amazing dance performance. and the peacocks open their green feathers to close and closes the curtains.

That was the beauty of animals and nature, all living creatures given by god has beauty and makes the world beautiful. We learnt that we are losing our beauty by slaughtering them day by day. We must try and preserve this beauty. Because, this is natural beauty

ALL THE LITTLE MINDS

I was in the eighth grade; I went to pick my little sister up from nursery. You can see me there peeping in every door step as I do not even have a single idea of where her class is. It was a tough job.

Firstly, I peeped into the music room. There was no sign of my sister but another kid with her mini piano. The whole class looked in awe seeing how she played twinkle twinkle little star perfectly on pitch and flowing with the music notes. I think she played better that young Beethoven.

No sign of her in the art room as well. But oh! What a beautiful painting. All on a mini canvas, in front of it was a cute little boy with a messy little apron. All with that little brush, a tooth brush and even his hand. What an imagination does these kids have?

There is seen no sister in the karate room. Oh boy! a kid swinging nunchakus like he was born swinging them. and even boke a wooden board with a bare kick! How strong he is, looks like baby Bruce lee

No sister dancing in the dance room. But a fluttering swan twirled upon the stage. All stars shone around her glamorous tutu in the shape of a pink flower. She took the spotlight of the stage making even the teachers wowed.

A play going on there in the drama room with no sister. the play was Goldilocks and the three bears. The expression and emotion of the little goldilocks, her falling off the chair felt like she really cried in pain. When she is older, I think I will watch her movie.

Finally, here I see my sister in the story cabin. At the front of the class talking about those brave knights, lost princesses, huge dragons, and wicked witches amazing all those kids. I clapped in a corner and she notices me, and rushes to hug me.

All the kids in all rooms were really talented, even you have your own talent that makes you stand out from the others.

MY LETTER TO PROTESTERS

123- Wilson Garden, Bengaluru- 560068

2/24/2023, 9:00 pm

Dear Protesters,

We all go on a pathway there

but we do not know the way,

These people guide us how and where

Till' what we do this day.

We all went through a pathway of learning as we were in our youth, without knowing where to start.

The guides are our teachers who help us find our way by teaching us from the basics to where we are now. Because of them, we are where we are right now. Our destination! Where we reach our success.

We now talk about people who invented new things, are popular, found businesses that are now reaching the globe etc. It is not the hard work of these people, in fact, they did nothing on their own. It is but the teachers of these provinces that deserve so much credit.

Because of them, you are in your smart position you have today. Wearing your suit and tie, pants, and boots. Walking around with your sunglasses and pride.

But instead of paying them back for what they have done, you protest against them and cut their pay. You guys offended their 24/7 hard work making them severely depressed and even killing them because of that.

If you guys continue this, you will find your next generation a pile of trash. With no teachers, how much would this gen take to know their name. It will take as much as you take to start an invention around-the-clock.

and what about the future, it will go नौ दो ग्यारह.

So, we request you to kindly stop what you are doing and let them free. For they are equal to your future

Regards,

Sana Twinkle.

Inspired by incident shown in THE HINDU newspaper

"Teacher killed while protests were going on"

MR. RAMATU AND HIS DATE PRODUCE

I was sitting in the shade of a tree with my granny. We chatter like this almost every day. One such day we were busy chatting when Mr. Ramatu, the date farmer came up to us to talk about his new produce. His kind of dates usually grow in the wintertime, when trees are clean. As of now, it is boiling hot summer. He says that the dates rotted. He fell on his knees wailing, " O lord of Harvest! For days and nights of prayers, why did you fail on me? I repent all my sins towards you, please forgive me. I fear my family sleeping hungry tonight. Even if it means going to the moon, please tell me what to do? I promise you; I will give sacrifices and be a better person from tomorrow. Just please help me this once". I do not get it, what did he do wrong? why did God fail on him? Questions and questions pop up in my head about Mr. Ramatu.

The next day, granny and me followed Mr. Ramatu to his farm. He starts by sowing the seeds, singing verses while doing so. Then, He prays and prays. He sings hymn after hymn. waiting for the plants to grow. and sleeps only at 11:00pm. Granny had known that he did not give proper nourishments for the plants and only prayed, thinking that the plants will grow. She then had a brilliant idea.

After that day, the plan was set. We went to Mr. Ramatu and said that we have spoken to the god that night. He said that you prayed a lot, but you never gave him water. so he was really thirsty and decided to teach you a lesson. You also did not give him some space. he was tackled by the other seeds. You also need a lot of patience because he takes time to adjust to the climate. While doing that, he also should continue praying.

Mr. Ramatu followed the instructions of God and got a ripe produce within a couple of months. He was so happy he hugged us and invited us for dinner. Then, he asked me how I spoke to God.

Then, we told him that god does not help you, but he is there to motivate you for you to do it yourself.

You were just praying to God and doing nothing else. That shows that you are fully dependent on God. You should consider yourself weak without God but you should also help God with the tasks you want him to do.

THE DARK ROOM

My name is Riddhi. I live in the beautiful village of my ancestors, it had tall, colorful trees with different shades of green around me. My world is full of vibrant colors and bright pathways all around me. We always see children playing around the rose bush,

Eating apples from the trees and making rangolis with flowers and leaves. I have a very good circle of friends, my best one being Sumitra. One day at recess, Me, Sumitra, and her brother Sundar were thinking of playing a game of Hide-and-seek. Sumitra was the seeker. We were all rounding about for places where we can hide until Sundar found a tall Banyan tree and hid behind it. I was rushing to find a place as I heard a Sumitra alarm that I had only 10 seconds left. I immediately went inside a rusty, old shed in fear of losing the game. Inside it, was pitch black. There was nothing in the room except for a few paints. Then I thought, "What to do with just a black room. Think, Riddhi. Think. The one thing I decided to do is paint the room with all the colors of the rainbow to reveal its good side. Then, I made home for many naughty parrots and gave each of them a name. One of those naughty little ones pecked a tiny hole with its beak and there I peeked. My eyes gave a closer look and there found Sumitra and Sundar running up closer and closer, step by step as if they are going in a cave. They found the shed and opened the little door and found me. I told her from head to toe about the rusty shed which turned into a magical place. We both loved it and called it 'The place of miracles'. In the modern days, we all just call it a colorful room but it will be a happy place for many kids at the bottom of your heart.

Moral

The same way Riddhi turned a bland, colorless shed into a magical place, we should find at least a gram of happiness even during the saddest of times.

www.ingramcontent.com/pod-product-compliance
Lightning Source LLC
LaVergne TN
LVHW061625070526
838199LV00070B/6576